WRITTEN BY
AMY FRITSCHE

Resilience

A SURVIVAL GUIDE FOR THE MODERN ACTOR

Cover images © Shutterstock.com

www.innovativeinkpublishing.com
Send all inquiries to:
4050 Westmark Drive
Dubuque, IA 52004-1840

CONTENTS

FOREWORD

I met Amy Fritsche at a conference in early 2020 (right before the world took a rather intense turn). In attending her presentation, I felt an immediate kinship with the views she was expressing. I could see that Amy approached the business of theatre with a mix of generosity, practicality, and passion that reminded me of how I work with singers.

As a reader of this book, you also can now be the beneficiary of Amy's finely honed insights.

One of the many things that sets *Resilience* apart is that Amy is the embodiment of "walking the walk." In writing this book, she interviewed countless professionals in our industry and boiled their wisdom down to practical advice that you can take away and use immediately.

More uniquely, she also auditioned and took class herself to experience what it's like to be in your shoes in a visceral way.

It's exceedingly rare in academia to have a professor like Amy who can combine the rigors of academic research with the real-world experience of how to navigate the industry as it stands now. Her willingness to put herself out there as an actor, director, and teacher gives you a golden opportunity to learn from the best.

My company and book are called *The Singing Athlete,* and I bring the worlds of neuroscience and athletic training into the voice studio. As a lover of the brain, there are several things that stood out to me in reading Amy's book. She emphasizes the human search for patterns and meaning; this neural impulse is one of the reasons why art is so satisfying to create and experience. It provides a framework for our existence.

The world of theatre can seem to be focused entirely on external validation (applause, reviews, etc.). In reading *Resilience,* you will learn invaluable strategies for developing *internal* awareness (known in the neuroscience world as *interoception*). Your internal map is an underappreciated area of artistic development, and it can lead you to a better ability to cope with stress and performance anxiety.

A sign of brain health is your ability to take in new information and change course if needed. In reading this book, you will gain a toolbox for the mental flexibility needed to thrive as an actor.

One of the keys to avoiding burnout in any career is a love of lifelong learning. In addition to being a great model of this principle, Amy gives you concise methods to find a path that will motivate you to keep building your craft and exploring new creative avenues.

The most important thing you can get out of reading Amy's book is a more balanced perspective. Drawing on her wealth of experience in different aspects of the field, she helps you zoom out and see how you fit into the gigantic puzzle that is the arts. You will take these lessons along with you for the rest of your life and throughout your performing journey.

Enjoy absorbing the wisdom contained in the following pages, and thank you for your dedication to storytelling.

Andrew Byrne (Author of *The Singing Athlete: Brain-Based Training for Your Voice*)

PREFACE

This book is a collection of stories, questions, and possibilities for actors and artists. I am an actor, director, choreographer, teacher, and creator—but not an expert. In fact, I'm not sure there *is* an expert in this field, as each artist's journey and version of success is unique. I've spent decades working as an artist, and, in developing this book, I spent the last few years interviewing professionals in New York City to shape the questions presented throughout. The intention of this book is to illuminate potential pathways, offering guideposts that will get you moving toward *your* version of success. It also aims to cultivate the inquisitive resilience needed to keep moving forward. Please remember that, as a fellow actor, I am going through this process alongside you. What resonates today may not be relevant tomorrow, so take the viewpoints shared here with a fine grain of salt. Find what works for you and throw the rest away.

We are storytellers. To be human is to tell ourselves stories about the world around us. As Brené Brown puts it, "Our minds are engineered to seek out patterns and assign meaning to them. Humans are a meaning-making species." Take, for example, my current experience: I'm sitting in a cozy coffee shop on the Upper West Side, composing this introduction, when a giant dog walks in. I love dogs immensely, so in *my* story, this large, Irish Wolfhound-sized dog bounding into the tinny coffee shop is a delightful surprise. But in *someone else's* story—someone who might be afraid of dogs—this same scene could be terrifying. Stories are how we tell ourselves our lives. They define who we are, what we like, who we like, what's acceptable, and what everything means. This is an essential concept to grasp because the story you tell yourself about your career—and your place in the industry—will profoundly influence your experience within the profession.

The goal of this book is to get to you to understand the reality of the industry. It is NOT my job or my goal to discourage you from your dreams. But it is my responsibility as a teacher and an actor to tell you the physical facts about the industry and let you make your own informed decision.

The reality of the business is—it's hard, amazing, easy, impossible, heart-wrenching, soul-crushing, and exhilarating, all at the same time. You can have years when you are on the top of the world, followed by the next ten+ years where you will not pay your bills by acting.

ACKNOWLEDGMENT

My special thanks goes to Darlene and David Fritsche, Ben Gregg, Lisa Kerfoot, Andrew Byrne, and the 70+ individuals I had the privilege of interviewing between 2022 and 2024. I also dedicate this book to my past students. Your passion for this industry inspires me every day, driving me to ensure that future students' journeys are even more rewarding.

About the Author

Amy Fritsche has worked with Fox Animations Studios, toured nationally with *Annie* and internationally in the world premiere of *Best Intentions* in London, England and at the Edinburgh Festival Fringe. She performed at Cleveland Play House in the world premiere of *These Mortal Hosts*. Regionally, she has performed at Phoenix Theatre, Arkansas Shakespeare Theatre, CATCO Theatre, Cleveland Public Theatre, Dobama Theatre, Porthouse Theatre, Mamai Theatre, and Odyssey Theatre in Los Angeles. Favorite roles include *Next to Normal* (Diana), *Arcadia* (Hannah Jarvis), *Superior Donuts* (Officer Randy), *9 to 5* (Violet), *As You Like It* (Rosalind), *A Little Night Music* (Countess Charlotte), *Annie* (Grace Farrell), *Penelopiad* (Penelope), and *Violet* (Violet). She received the 2015 Cleveland Critics Circle Theatre Award for Best Actress in a Musical for her portrayal of Violet and the 2018 Cleveland Critics Circle Theatre Award for Best Actress in a Musical for her portrayal of Diana in *Next to Normal*. She is a proud member of SAG/AFTRA, AGVA, and AEA.

As a director choreographer, she has directed in NYC and regionally; some of her favorite shows include *The Crucible, Irene's Vow, Heathers, All Shook Up, RENT, The Mystery of Edwin Drood, Anything Goes, Into the Woods, Side Show, The Marvelous Wonderettes, Hot Mikado, The Crucible,* and *Legally Blonde*. She gave a TedX on "Theater as a medium of Social Change" through the lens of Irena's Vow.

She is currently associate professor of acting and musical theatre at Kent State University. She was the winner of the 2020 Distinguished Teaching Award. Amy Fritsche earned her Master of Fine Arts in musical theatre from San Diego State University graduating Phi Kappa Phi. She earned a Bachelor of Fine Arts in acting from the University of Southern California where she received the James and Nony Doolittle Award. She has also studied at Yale University, American Academy of Dramatic Arts, and Beverly Hills Playhouse. Amy has taught acting, directing, and musical theatre at Southeast Missouri State University, acting at San Diego State University and The La Jolla Playhouse and taught dance at numerous dance studios in Arizona and California. For more information please go to amyfritsche.com.

THE SELF

Introduction

A Little about Me—OR the Story I Tell Myself about My Life in the Arts and the Reason I Am Writing This Book

This whole project is a love letter to my younger self and a guide to navigate the performing arts industry.

Let me share a quick story about my journey in the arts.

I first got into dance because of my "learning disorder" (more about this later), and, when I was a preteen, I had two events that changed the trajectory of my life. The first happened when I was splitting my time between competitive dance and the ballet world. I found myself at the Joffrey Ballet School in NYC, studying intensely, while also preparing for a national dance competition. Amid all this, I had an emotional fallout with my primary dance teacher of many years and sustained a lower back injury so severe that it forced me to stop dancing full-time. After the injury, my family and I went to see *Blood Brothers* on Broadway. By then, I'd seen plenty of musicals, but something about this show struck me in a way that made me want to pursue musical theatre. When I returned to my hometown in Arizona, I made the switch from dancing to musical theatre—a decision that would set the course for my future.

During my time in Phoenix, I was fortunate to book Theatre Leagues Tour of *Annie* and work with Fox Animation Studios. From there, I was accepted into the University of Southern California's (USC) BFA Acting program—though on a conditional basis. What that meant was I had to go to tutoring and take a special class to teach me how to study and learn time management tools. I also had to uphold a C+ average and above in all my classes for the first year. I absolutely loved my time at USC, and I definitely learned how to act. However, I was surprised to realize that, despite all the training, I felt I had learned very little about the actual *business* of acting.

My childhood best friend was a successful working actor while I was attending USC. Both during and after graduation, I was determined to pursue a career in film and television, and Southern California seemed like the obvious place to make that happen. My success in Phoenix, combined with watching my friend navigate the industry, gave me the illusion that "making it" would be easy. But I eventually realized that her path—and the luck, talent, and hard work that shaped it—was uniquely her own. My navigation of Hollywood was entirely different.

In my early 20s, I struggled to find work as an actor. Upon reflection, I think there were a lot of contributing factors. Luck and timing certainly played a role. But I also lacked the resilience and coping mechanisms to handle my "failures." I was highly impressionable, and the obsessive "making it" mindset, which so often consumes young actors, became all-consuming. I fell into the trap of external validation, from where I derived my self-worth and identity.

I think my desire to be chosen followed me into every audition room. I also struggled with some of the harsh and often cosmetic aspects of casting. In the early 2000s, I didn't fit the body type that Hollywood was seeking. I was told by my agent and acting teachers that I either needed to gain 20 pounds to play the "best friend" role or lose 20 pounds to become the ingénue. I got tired of twisting myself into what I thought other people wanted.

After years of figuratively running into a brick wall, I decided to leave the industry. The tipping point came after I was cast in a pilot episode for a law-themed television show, only for the show to be canceled on the first day of shooting.

Looking back, maybe I should have pushed through and kept fighting for a place in the industry. But at the time, I didn't have the resilience or mindset necessary to keep going.

So, what did I do after that? I tried a variety of different careers.
I ran my own massage company. I randomly became a corporate travel agent for a few years. I even managed a multi-million-dollar business. And, along the way, I fell in love and settled into the nine-to-five grind. But after all that, you know what I learned?

I was still unfulfilled.

Then one day, my mom came across a listing for a musical theatre summer production at a local community college and encouraged me to audition. For various reasons, I couldn't perform in the show, but the director eventually asked if I'd be interested in assisting him and choreographing the production.

At that point, I hadn't been involved in the creative arts for four years. When I had walked away from acting, I was bitter about the industry and my place in it. But working on this show—directing and choreographing—rekindled something inside me.

It reminded me how much I love teaching—something I've been doing, on and off, since I was 16.

After some time and discernment, I became passionate about the possibility of teaching at the collegiate level. I hoped to impact young people like my mentors had impacted me. The journey of graduate school and teaching allowed me to experience firsthand how to become a resilient and sustained working artist. I have the honor of teaching at a nationally recognized theatre program, while also cultivating a robust acting career on stage, performing with nationally recognized regional theatres. I have also directed and choreographed shows both regionally and in New York City.

Over the past few years, through interviews with directors, casting directors, agents, managers, and actors, I saw firsthand how no one's journey through this industry is the same. Each person has faced their own struggles and hurdles to overcome. And they all continue to evolve their own ever-changing definition of success in the entertainment industry.

The following pages are guides to help you navigate and create resilience.

Unique, Not Special

Merriam-Webster's definition of "unique" is "being the only one of its kind; unlike anything else." There is only one of you. The path that brought you here and the experiences that have shaped your life are entirely your own. But that doesn't mean you're *special*.

According to *Webster*, "special" means "better, greater, or otherwise different from what is usual." We may be special to the people who love us, but in this industry, you are not special. You are not "better or greater" than anyone else in the room. You are unique. Your *uniqueness* is what you have to offer. It is the only thing that can truly set you apart in this industry and will be the guiding force as you move forward.

What is truly unique about you?

What do you bring to the room that no one else does?

Worth and Worthy

What is your definition of worth?

One definition of *worth* in the *Webster* dictionary is "moral or personal value."

If you move to NYC, Atlanta, or LA, the basic expectation is every actor is good, and, I repeat, every actor is good. So being a good actor is not your worth. Being praised for a good performance is not your worth. Winning awards is not your worth. Being on Broadway or starring in TV or movies is not your worth. Your worth is made up by the totality of who you are. No one can grant you worth because you got a job, but it is the owning and knowing of the worth that might get you the job. (Yes, I know the duality of that is complicated.)

It broke my heart seeing an acquaintance of mine posting a picture of themselves standing on a Broadway stage during a backstage tour and posted that one day they would be worthy of being on this stage. This is a trap. No job, no location, no experience can grant you your worth. The beauty of theatre, film, and television is that one day the gig will be gone. So, if you get your worth from that project, what will you do when it ends?

Where your worth comes from is ultimately up to you. You don't have to be working to still be an artist, to be worthy. Your worth originates from the small actions you do every day. Interaction with strangers, having a great time with friends, going on an adventure, walking around the city you love, spending time with your loved ones, or taking in a museum, art, or sporting event. Your worth comes from the small actions that compose your life, not some grand job. Jobs end, and, when they do ultimately, you still must deal with the part of you that did not feel worthy to begin with.

Outside of the arts, what makes you feel worthy?

What aspects within the arts make you feel worthy?

What in your life defines you outside of a job?

Do you seek outside validation for your worth? Is social media a place where you get your worth?

Can you put your phone down, shut down your computer, and discover worth in the small things versus likes, shares, and external validation? Start small, try it for a few minutes a day. It is a muscle worth flexing.

Dreams and Defined Success

What are your dreams?

Have you ever deeply desired to date a certain person, try a particular food, or travel to an exotic destination, only to find that once you achieve these goals, they don't solve your problems, fill you up, or affirm you? The tricky thing about dreams is that once we achieve one, there's always another goal waiting to be reached. We're wired to constantly search for the next challenge—the next opportunity for growth, enrichment, and achievement. Social media only amplifies this cycle, constantly feeding our desire for more.

That said, this doesn't mean you shouldn't dream or have desires. Dreams are important. They define our internal compass and give us a sense of direction for where we want our lives to go.

What is success?

The best definition of success I have ever come across is from legendary UCLA basketball coach John Wooden who said that "*Success* is peace of mind that is the direct result of self-satisfaction in knowing you did your best to become the best that you are capable of becoming." The reason this definition resonates with me is that Wooden emphasizes the actions you can take help you determine your success instead of needing validation from someone else. It is not something external you can achieve; it is a moment-to-moment evaluation of your own effort, honesty, and drive.

Looking at this definition of success, I want you now to evaluate your dreams, your worth, your uniqueness, and your values. Could you be a fulfilled artist and human by holding yourself accountable every day? How would you grow as a person and artist if you were only moving forward based on your own momentum versus external validations?

The Why

Why did you decide to declare to the world that you will be become an actor, an artist, a performer, dancer, singer, and so on?

Knowing why you entered this industry can help reconnect you to your *why*—the driving force that keeps you moving forward, even in the face of setbacks along your professional journey. A colleague, Mark Enticknap, who works as an actor and social worker in the UK, helped articulate some of the driving factors as to why people *might* choose to create a life in the arts.

Some of these reasons include:
- The performing arts provided a safe space where you could be yourself without fear of judgment.
- It got you attention and helped shape your sense of status or identity. Through the arts, you received compliments, applause, praise, and affirmations you might not have otherwise received.
- It offered escapism. Perhaps you've been acting and pretending your whole life—hiding who you really are and putting on a front. You may believe you'll be successful as an actor because you've spent so much time disguising your true self.
- It acted as a means to work out a psychological difficulty you may be experiencing in life. (*Note: Acting is not therapy. While the creative arts can be therapeutic, acting is NOT a substitute for therapy.*)
- The craft itself intrigues and compels you. You are drawn to explore the mindset of others and authentically tell their stories. You feel it's your vocation, and you're good at it.

Perhaps some of these reasons might be applicable to you, and perhaps some of them aren't. Regardless, I think it's important to understand why you were drawn to this industry. Understanding and reigniting the genesis of what led you into the profession can help sustain you through the inevitable challenges that come with this industry. Knowing the why behind it will help you understand yourself more. This can help you bring your whole self to your work.

Personal Story, "My Why"

In second grade, I was diagnosed with a learning disability. I have severe dyslexia with a few other challenges sprinkled in for good measure. The two options put forward to my parents were to put me in the Special Education classes or get me a tutor. My parents elected the tutor. From second through the eighth grade, I worked with an amazing tutor for five days-a-week, every week, throughout the school year. I struggled relating to some of my fellow classmates. I was branded the weird, stupid kid for the majority of my elementary school and junior high days. The one place I felt safe, seen, and was tremendously successful was in the dance studio. It was the place where I thrived. Throughout my years performing, I have been reintegrating the safety and validation I felt on stage into my daily life. While I've had my struggles with the industry, I think I've ultimately been drawn to the arts because it's helped me gain confidence and reimagine myself, and, most importantly, it's provided a sense of community.

Where to start: It's time to dream and start asking yourself some really hard questions. (Please note that the answers may change from day to day/year to year, etc.) Right now, where you are, wherever you're reading or listening to this, I want you to ask yourself the questions listed below. These answers will be a guide to the rest of this book. PLEASE know that you should ask these questions throughout your professional journey as they're likely to change at various points in your life and career.

What does a successful *career* look like to you? Make sure you cover everything such as the types of jobs you will work on, the roles you will play, the people you will work with, and money you will earn. Get specific in writing down all the details. Whatever you write down will be uniquely yours. I have done this exercise with hundreds of students and have received an exponential number of different answers.

Now ask yourself what does a successful *LIFE* look like? This should be different than career. It should include all facets of life, including travel, food, clothes, animals, partners, friends, community, health, and what brings you joy.

Now how does your career and life intersect? How do they build off each other? How do they complement each other? How do they clash with each other? You don't have to solve these questions; just notice what is driving you.

Take this list and be willing to go one step further: Ask yourself *why*. WHY? This is a question I ask myself and my students often. If we can understand the *why* behind our desires, we can better assess whether what we think we want will truly fulfill that deeper need.

So, why is that your version of success? If you achieve it, what will it define or accomplish in your life? Why is this specific outcome your idea of a successful life?

What happens if you don't achieve any of it? What do you imagine your life will look like then? Why do you believe these particular things equal success?

What if all your dreams were to come true? What would that feel like? What underlying need would be fulfilled? Why would achieving everything you desire equal success?

Now, for the tough question: How do you create a successful life *even if* you don't achieve these goals? What does the quality of life you want to live look like, regardless of outcomes?

Are you willing to let go of this version of success, if life presents you with different opportunities? Are you open to releasing childhood dreams and creating new ones at this stage of your life?

The irony of life is that you might achieve everything on your list, only to find it doesn't bring the fulfillment you expected. Or you might get nothing on the list and still feel completely successful. There are no set rules. It's important to take time, periodically, to redefine success on your own terms. This way, you can move forward with confidence.

Actor: Being versus Doing

Being an actor and artist is not about the gigs you have done, the roles you performed, the auditions you have been on, or the agents you have. Being an actor is a way of life; it is how you show up in everything you do. It is a way of being inquisitive and empathetic, of engaging in the world with love, understanding, and curiosity. It is a passion that flows through you and a drive that ignites your being. So be an actor every day. Find time for yourself to do the craft you love even if it is in your own room, on the computer, or in the streets. It's about filling up the well of inspiration for yourself and expressing it—even the most mundane activities. It could even appear in the way you pour your latte, engage with your colleagues, and show up to your world. There is no aptitude test or bar/medical exam that grants you permission be an actor—only *you* can do that. It is a claiming of the essence that is inside of you that no one can take away. Being an actor cannot be won or lost because you did or didn't book a job. If you claim you are an actor, scream it to the stars and embody it. Being an actor is not granted by a paycheck; it is granted by knowing the drive and passion you have in your heart to express yourself.

I enjoy the history and etymology of the word "actor." In Middle English, *actour* meant "doer," borrowed from the Latin *actor*, meaning "one who causes to move, one who does." The word *artist* comes from the Middle French *artiste*, meaning "a person practicing a craft." Being an actor is what you are doing or causing to move, in yourself, and in the people around you. Being an artist is about practicing the craft of acting: an active preparation and a way of engaging with the world.

What do you need to do to fully believe that you are an actor and an artist?

How can you grant yourself the permission to fully own your artistic essence?

Human First

I once heard a casting director say that if given the choice between speaking with an actor who eats, breathes, and sleeps acting or one who has just returned from backpacking around the world, they would always choose the backpacker. Why? Because, in their view, the backpacker has experienced the world and will bring a fresh perspective—something different from an actor who is solely immersed in the industry.

I interviewed over seventy professionals to get their take on the current state of the industry. In these conversations, I asked each of them about the best and worst advice they'd ever received. A recurring theme was the age-old recommendation: "If you can see yourself doing anything other than this, go do it." The reactions to this advice were sharply divided—some actors agreed, while others violently rejected it.

The hard truth of the business is you might have to do anything and everything other than acting to be able to have a life as an actor. Only 2% of actors worldwide make a living solely from acting, and at any given time, 90% are out of work. I'm sharing these statistics not to scare you, but to give you a clearer picture of the reality you're entering. You will need to become a multi-hyphenate actor. The *Cambridge Dictionary* defines multi-hyphenate "as someone who does several different jobs, especially in the entertainment industry."

The other jobs you take on can be key to both your happiness and your long-term sustainability in the industry. The most successful actors I spoke with all mentioned the importance of finding work that offers the flexibility to pursue acting, while also providing financial stability and the ability to live a full, balanced life in the city they choose. For some, this means serving, bartending, nannying, teaching, working 9–5 in tech, retail, coffee shops, or even baking. There's no *one* right job—it's about finding the work that supports your well-being, so you can keep pursuing what truly makes your soul sing.

A key thing to remember is it is possible to find a single job that can cover all your bills. It may take time, but the idea that you need multiple jobs to survive isn't necessarily true. Early on, it might feel that way, but eventually, you'll find the one job that can support you financially. Also, if your current job starts to drain your energy or stifle your spirit, it's time to look for something else. (Obviously, easier said than done, especially depending on the state of the economy.) Don't fall into the trap of thinking you have to stay in a job just because it's paying the bills. Remember, this job is meant to support your life and your craft, not deplete you. If it's taking too much from you, you won't have the energy or inspiration to give your best to your artistry.

Please remember that being an artist or having training as an actor means you possess a wide range of transferable skills. These include:

- **Communication** (active listening)
- **Teamwork** (working in an ensemble)
- **Narrative understanding and detailed analysis** (script analysis)
- **Emotional intelligence and empathy** (stepping into a character's shoes)
- **On-your-feet problem-solving** (yes, and)
- **Working under pressure** (opening night)
- **Time management** (early is on time, on time is late, late is fired)
- **Strong work ethic** (tech week)
- **Troubleshooting** (when your scene partner forgets a line)
- **Critical thinking** (character analysis)
- **Creativity** (the entire artistic process)

These "soft skills" are highly valued across many industries. Don't sell yourself short by thinking you lack skills—you have a toolbox full of them!

If you don't know where to start with finding a job, perhaps take some time to reflect on your interests and skills. What are your hobbies? What interests you? What do you gravitate toward when you are not acting? What else made you curious as a child? What are some things you have always wanted to do? There are a variety of hobbies, from the outdoors, crafts, games-puzzles, word games, musical hobbies, cooking, brewing, and volunteering. These hobbies will possibly help you find another job, and they will also help you build a community outside of the performing arts.

In our society, one of the first questions we ask kids is—"What do you want to be when you grow up?" I've seen many pictures of my friend's children holding up signs going into first and second grade proclaiming that when they grow up they want to be in X, Y, or Z occupation. This is great in theory, but I question if we are *perpetuating the idea that what we want to be is the person who we will become.*

This line of thinking often carries over into adulthood, particularly in the small talk that occurs on airplanes or in waiting rooms. When meeting someone new, the first question we're often asked is, *"What do you do for a living?"* Either a reluctant "ohhh…," indicating the subtext that you must wait tables for a living. (Side note, there is also nothing wrong with waiting tables. We live in a culture that devalues the service industry.) Or the dreaded follow-up question, "Have I seen you in anything?"

Even in academia, I've experienced similar reactions. In university-wide research meetings, when I mention that I teach theatre, there's often an underlying skepticism or judgment. They assume that teaching theatre must be fun and easy, with the implication that what we do isn't a valid profession or considered legitimate research.

These moments can be difficult, because one of the main aspects of being an actor is auditioning, and, therefore, the opportunity to perform can be elusive. I saw this firsthand when interviewing actors in New York City toward the end of the COVID-19 pandemic. I observed that it was hard for them to disassociate their identity from their job. It's tough to say that you're *an actor* while the only thing you're doing is submitting self-tapes into the void.

So, the question arises, if you are not your job, then who are you?

I would love to change the culture and eliminate the question of "What do you want to do when you grow up?" Instead, I would ask "What type of person do you want be?" What are your core values that you want to show up in everything you do? How do you want to meet the world? What type of life do you want to cultivate?

> Who are you if you are not your job?
>
> What type of person do you want to be?

> What are your core values that you want to show up in everything you do?
>
> How do you want to meet the world?
>
> What type of life do you want to cultivate?

Creating a Life in the Big City

Creating a life in a new city takes time. From speaking with other actors and reflecting on my own experiences, I've found that it usually takes at least three to five months to truly settle in. You have to find a job, secure an apartment, locate your gym, decide if you need a therapist, and build your social circle. Personally, I've moved to three different cities as an adult where I didn't know anyone, and I can tell you, making new friends as an adult is harder than it sounds!

You might be lucky and land in a city where you already have a group of friends or fellow recent graduates. Or, you might arrive knowing absolutely no one. But if you're willing to embrace the challenge of being the "new kid," most major cities are full of opportunities to meet people. There are plenty of ways to get started—attending dance or acting classes, hanging around after a theatre show to meet fellow audience members, taking up a new hobby, using apps to find meet-ups, or attending faith-based services. All of these are great ways to begin building a community.

During research for this book, multiple actors I talked to spoke about their feelings when they first moved to NYC. They disclosed how much they originally hated it! However, once they moved to a different neighborhood, met new roommates, or rented a new apartment, they began to love it. Finding a place in the city that serves as your homebase will help you thrive. It will translate into your self-tapes and your auditions. One recommendation I have is to try subletting for a few months in different locations around your new city. This way you can begin to find out what part of your new location speaks to you.

To be a whole actor, you first have to be a whole person. Taking the time to build your community and create a stable life outside of acting will directly impact your work. Finding hobbies you enjoy and places where you can pursue them will enrich your life and contribute to your overall sense of wellness. It's unrealistic to expect acting to provide 100% of your enjoyment and purpose. The craft is important, but it's just one part of a fulfilling life.

Go explore the city you live in. Find the local coffee shop, grocery store, bar, or restaurant. Most major cities like NYC have great parks and museums. When I lived in Los Angeles I would either spend my days at the beach or I would memorize lines at the La Brea tarpits. I enjoyed it because it was a respite to the city life and let me escape into nature. Try new things when you are in the city! Do some research! Many cities have free nights or half price days to museums, farmers markets, outdoor concerts, and local fairs. Find these for yourself so you have new places to explore and to meet people.

Revisit your answers from 'The Why' and reflect on how they connect to the type of LIFE you want.

How does living in your city of choice help you create that life?

Is there anything you need to change or add to feel more fulfilled in your current city?

The Mirror

Self-reflection is an important part of being an actor. If we aren't willing to regularly assess where we are—both as people and as artists—our growth will stagnate. I cannot stress enough the importance of mental and physical health in this self-reflection. Whether you're doing eight shows a week or working twelve to fourteen-hour days on set, it takes an immense amount of will and energy. But so does sending out videos and attending —two to ten auditions a week and sometimes not ever hearing anything back for months (or even) years on end. Building resilience is key to navigating these tough times, and there are strategies you can put in place to buffer against the inevitable disappointment.

One of the most important buffers is creating a fulfilling life outside of acting—establishing a life in the city you live in, cultivating relationships, and pursuing interests that nourish you. Another is developing a solid routine for nutrition and physical activity. Personally, I've learned that when I'm feeling lost, worried, or discouraged, my tendency is to reach for junk food. While it may offer a temporary escape, I always end up feeling worse afterward. It's that old saying—*misery loves company*. But I've found that when I can redirect that energy, whether by going for a walk or working out, I feel much better afterward, both physically and emotionally. I know that my body functions better and my mind is clearer when I eat foods that support my overall health.

I'm not a nutritionist, but I'd always recommend doing your own research or consulting one to understand what your body needs to perform at its highest level. I also encourage you to find a workout routine that works for you and fits your budget. Maintaining physical stamina and supporting your body is crucial in this industry, and it's essential for keeping a balanced life.

Mentally, I'm a strong advocate for working with a competent therapist. To be an actor is to process the lives of characters who are experiencing a wide spectrum of emotions and experiences. Acting is an inherently vulnerable, emotional endeavor, and, at times, we are asked to bare our soul both in performance and perhaps especially in the audition room. Receiving a barrage of rejection over an extended period can be demoralizing, so having someone to help you process those emotions is invaluable. If therapy isn't an option right now, journaling can also be a powerful tool. Writing down your thoughts and the stories you're telling yourself helps you process feelings and gain clarity. Friends can also be an excellent source of support, but it's important to have people around you who understand the rollercoaster that is the acting life.

Ultimately, it's about finding your own tools to navigate this unpredictable and sometimes challenging journey. Whether through physical, mental, or emotional practices, taking care of yourself will help you stay resilient and continue growing as both a person and an artist.

How can you improve your eating or workout habits?

What needs to change in order for you to sustain being an actor?

Can you find someone to talk to regarding the peaks and valleys of being an actor?

Do you have a support system to help you through this journey? If you don't, what do you need to put into place to cultivate one?

Gratitude and Celebration

The hashtag #Grateful has become ubiquitous on social media. However, gratitude and celebration are an important component in the road of being an artist. While #Grateful may be everywhere in our culture, it can contribute to the climate of toxic positivity. There needs to be a balance of harnessing gratitude for what we've accomplished while also being forthright about the reality that not everything works out. It's a fine line to navigate.

As I've mentioned before, I spoke with many professional actors during the process of writing this book. In these conversations, several actors admitted that they're hesitant to acknowledge or celebrate their accomplishments because they fear it will bring bad luck. They're being superstitious. The thought is, if they're happy with their audition, the callback, the agent, the manager, and so on, and if they enjoy or celebrate those achievements, then they will jinx themselves somehow. This mindset is understandable, but not embracing the small victories prevents us from acknowledging how far we have come in our journey. I know I've often felt guilty or self-conscious about celebrating my successes, worried that it might come off as bragging. But celebrating those moments is a crucial buffer against the negativity that often surrounds us. It's important to know why and how you celebrate your achievements. It's also important to honor these accomplishments with those who will truly cherish these moments. Who is that person in your life right now?

One day during my time in NYC, I was conversing with a dear friend on the subway when he was bemoaning how many auditions he had scheduled for that day. He was honestly overwhelmed by the number of self-tapes he needed to record, the time it would take, the money he'd need to spend renting the dance studio, and, above all, the short turnaround time for these auditions—less than forty-eight hours. While we were packed into the train car full of people, I began to laugh because everything he described would have been a cause for celebration ten years ago. In this moment, he failed to recall that his younger self would view his current circumstances as a dream come true. He became a desired actor in NYC spending his day filled with art going to auditions and callbacks for shows.

Take a moment to remember that right now, you might be living your past dream—or someone else's current dream. Whether it's being accepted into a musical theatre program, moving to a big city like NYC for the first time, getting your own apartment, attending an in-person audition, filming a self-tape, going to a dance class or voice lesson, or having a breakthrough in an acting class—all of these moments are goals you had or moments that many people aspire to but can't achieve for one reason or another. Whether it's performing at a local theatre, opening a show at a theme park or cruise ship, filming a commercial, being an extra on a set, booking a major project, performing at a regional theatre, or even on a Broadway stage—these opportunities aren't guaranteed.

At some point in your life, you likely wanted to be exactly where you are right now, doing exactly what you're doing. And in these moments, it's important to acknowledge and celebrate with deep, genuine gratitude that you are DOING THE WORK. You, for one moment, accomplished a dream.

Take a moment to look back—what path has brought you to this moment?

Are there past wins you need to celebrate?

How do you plan on doing this?

What past dreams are you currently living?

Support/Judgment/Shit-Talking

Finding a strong support system is essential for thriving both mentally and physically in this industry. The kind of support you need can vary, but it's important to recognize the different ways it shows up. Support might come from people you trust during tough times, from those who lift you up, from those who encourage you to take better care of yourself, or from those who challenge you to do better.

In an industry where criticism can often outweigh praise, it's easy to fall into the trap of tearing others down. But that kind of negativity can be harmful, and it's important to consciously surround yourself with those who build you up instead.

It can be easy to disparage someone when they're booking gigs and you're not, or when they have something you think you deserve. Another contagious virus in the world and particularly in the performing arts that can break a cast or even a group of friends *is gossip*. At some point, we've all felt the sting of being the target of rumors or innuendos. The heartbreak that comes from discovering someone you cared about has spoken ill of you can be devastating. Yet, it's all too easy to get caught up in that behavior and join the group mentality of tearing others down behind their backs.

When building your support system, it's crucial to surround yourself with people who lift you up, not those who tear you down. I've found that, if possible, it can be helpful to make friends who have nothing to do with the performing arts—people you can share your victories with and who will support you through thick and thin. It can be incredibly difficult to live with or be close friends with someone who is "making it" while you feel stuck. In this industry, jealousy is real, and it can erode the foundation of even the strongest relationships. Combating jealousy takes a concerted effort.

One solution is to focus on where your value lies and what you uniquely have to offer the world. It's also important to be honest with yourself about your emotions. Personally, I've found that my jealousy of others' success often stems from my own insecurities and fears of not being good enough. I realize I'm comparing where I am to where I think I *should* be. When I step back far enough, I remember that I truly want those around me to succeed.

One of my favorite stories I tell my students is a cautionary tale about being mindful of where and to whom you complain about your circumstances in the performing arts. The story goes like this: An actor had a rough audition, everything seemed to go wrong, and they did not know that they were the last person to be seen that day. They were upset because the accompanist did not play their music right, the casting director never looked up from their paper, and a litany of other quibbles about why the audition didn't go well. Afterwards, they stopped by a store to buy something quickly and proceeded to walk to the train. The whole way to the train on the phone they vented about the casting director and all the things that went wrong. What they didn't realize was that the very casting director they had just auditioned for was walking right behind them and overheard every word. That casting director then contacted the actor's agent and that actor never had the chance to audition for that casting director again. The lesson here is simple: be very careful when, where, and to whom you air your grievances about this industry. Only complain about someone in this industry in your closet, to your closest friend or family, with the doors closed. It does not matter the size of the city; you never know who is listening.

When in your life have you torn down a friend, colleague, or participated in gossip?

Pinpoint what the underlying reason was for your choice?

Can you make amends and find a way to make it right?

How would you judge someone who said disparaging comments about you behind your back?

Are you jealous of others?

What is the underlying cause of the jealousy?

Has your jealousy stopped you from supporting those around you?

How can you remedy this?

Snuggling Up with Failure and Fear

One thing I can almost guarantee in any industry, but specifically in the performing arts, is that at some time or the other your heart will be broken, and, worse, beyond broken, it will be decimated. The job will not come, the agent will say no, you will be replaced mid-show, or you will get down to the last two people in the casting process but don't fit the costume. There are a myriad of other setbacks, and all of them can feel devastating. One possible way to navigate through these challenges is to embrace them! Be willing to sit with what you wished and longed for and give yourself permission to grieve. Through my multiple interviews I asked actors how they deal with fear and failure. Here are some of the suggestions.

- Control what you can control and approach it like an experiment. Analyze all the things you did and see if there was anything you could improve upon. Make the changes and implement them into your next audition.
- Embrace the sting. Give yourself a set amount of time to cry, yell, and process the anger and the disappointment. Go to the gym, go for a walk, or talk to a safe person who is willing to sit in it with you. Once that allotted time is over, go out and do things that bring you joy and remind you why you love being an artist.
- Book the room and not the audition. Do the work, leave it in the space, and GO on with your day. Make sure you have a full day lined up so that there is no time to worry about "how it went."
- Make art out of the disappointment, dance it out, sing it out, and act it out. Turn the hurt into something beautiful.
- Have a group of friends who will pick you up and keep you going while also holding you accountable for your actions.
- Go back to your full life. Your job is to audition. Life is not that job, or that audition, *your life is your life.*
- If your audition was for a film or television role, make yourself watch the episode that you were ultimately being considered for. This way you can see who they picked, and perhaps you can begin to evaluate why they may have chosen the other actor over you.
- ***It's Not Personal***. Managing expectations is key, and understanding what you can and cannot control is crucial. You're in control of how much time

you spend preparing for your audition. You control the hours you dedicate to practicing, dancing, and singing in class, building your skills for that opportunity. You control the quality of your self-tape and how you present yourself in the callback room. But everything else—the decisions made on the other side of the table—is beyond your control. It's vital to manage your expectations around this. You're also in control of what you can change about your approach. The next important step is being willing to change. You can't dig your heels in and think you're entitled to the role or that you deserve it because of your talent or experience. That mentality doesn't fly in this industry. I can promise you, there's always someone out there who is willing to adapt and improve. While you're feeling dejected, they're taking the steps necessary to succeed.

- A rough estimate in this industry is that you'll get one callback for every hundred auditions. Of course, this success rate can vary depending on where you are in your career, but the takeaway from this statistic is clear: Rejection is inevitable. It's up to you to decide how you'll respond to it. Be honest with yourself: Is this role truly right for you? If you believe it is but you still aren't being cast, ask yourself what you can do to improve. Do you need more voice lessons? More dance training? Is it a matter of body type, or are there factors beyond your control that you simply can't change?

- Getting solid, constructive, and objective feedback is crucial. While this feedback may not always come from the casting director, it can come from trusted sources like your agent or acting coach. Being honest with yourself is important, but it's equally essential to build relationships with people you trust—people who can offer honest, insightful feedback about your work.

- Beware of your coping mechanisms. Drinking, binge eating, drugs, doom scrolling, endlessly comparing yourself to others, and so on are all recipes for future failure. How can you turn that energy into something productive or positive? Or at the very least something that's actually about extending some kindness to yourself?

- **KEEP GOING**. If this is really what you want to do, you are going to receive rejection at some point in your career. It is at the very least partially your responsibility to choose how you will respond when facing those challenges or rejections.

- Embrace "Hope," but not in the passive emotion of "I hope I get it" but rather in the way that Crystal Bryce, Associate Director of Research in the Hope Center, defines it: "Hopeful people are able to set goals, identify ways to reach their goals and feel as though they can do the work to achieve those goals."

- Luck factors into any equation of success. Success usually amounts to a great deal of hard work, while also having the opportunity to **be at the right place at the right time**: BECAUSE EVEN IF YOU GET THE GIG, THERE ARE SO MANY THINGS THAT HAVE TO GO RIGHT FOR YOU TO HAVE SUCCESS! A GOOD CAST, A GOOD DIRECTOR, GOOD AUDIENCES, CRITICAL RECEPTION. Doing the work is the bare minimum because a ton of other stuff that's out of your control must "go right" to succeed in this insane industry.
- You never truly fail; you only learn. What defines you is not how many times you've tried, but how many times you get back up.

What strategies resonated with you?

How will you approach your next setback?

How can you take care of yourself when the next "no" comes?

Walking Away

Everyone one wants the gig, but, once we have it, we might not always want to keep it. In this industry, there's a prevailing belief in scarcity—that if we walk away from a job, an agent, or a manager, we may never get another opportunity. **But do not stay in an abusive situation.** Only you can define what abuse looks like for you, and only you can weigh the positives against the negatives.

I came of age in the dance world, where you weren't allowed to take off your pointe shoes unless there was blood on the floor. While that created a high tolerance for pain, I'm not sure it fostered healthy boundaries for my well-being. A friend of mine worked with a choreographer who was so abusive, they stopped dancing for a full year after the gig. They were harassed, belittled, and stayed in the job out of fear that speaking up would mean they'd never work again. Eventually, they took control by never auditioning for that person again—even when major projects were involved.

You have to be the one to determine if a job or a role is harming you. Will the choreography in an eight-show week break you physically? Is it worth singing through illness because there aren't enough understudies? Only you can decide when to step away or say no. You must weigh the short-term consequences against the long-term impact.

I know an actor who has permanent vocal damage because they were required to sing when they were sick. Another actor sustained a knee injury during a stage fight because they were afraid to speak up. That injury took them out of the show for good. I know of a show where the producing organization prioritized the shoes over the actors—despite the fact that the shoes were literally breaking the actors' ankles. There is a fine line between being "uncomfortable" with something and allowing it to physically or emotionally hurt you.

Was there ever a time when you should have walked away from a gig? What kept you from walking away?

In the future, what steps can you take to prioritize your emotional and physical well-being over a job?

Changing Your Mind

It's okay to change your mind. In our society, and especially in the world of the performing arts, the idea of quitting or altering your course is often frowned upon. Those who take the time to carefully consider major life decisions can be seen as indecisive or lacking conviction. However, I believe that self-reflection and the courage to change direction are essential to healthy vocational growth and personal well-being.

Let's be honest: Changing your mind often comes with a stigma. "Quitters" are frequently portrayed as failures in the media, which can create pressure into staying with acting (or any profession) when their heart is no longer in it. This mindset can trap people in careers and prevent them from exploring other opportunities where their skills and talents could truly flourish.

When interviewing one of my former students, they said, "I wish someone had told me it was okay to do something other than theatre." I've had students afraid to share with me that they were switching majors because they didn't want to disappoint me, or worse, feared I might shame them for changing their minds. Let me be clear: I would *never* do that, and no one has the right to make you feel ashamed for seeking a path that will bring you greater fulfillment.

I celebrate anyone who has the courage to pivot, to choose a career that brings them more joy, satisfaction, or alignment with their values. There are countless careers out there and many different paths where everything you've learned on stage, in the classroom, and backstage can be applied. In fact, many of the people I've interviewed—myself included—have left the performing arts at one point. Some came back, and others didn't. And you know what? That's *okay!*

If you decide to pursue something else, you are still an artist. Your artistic spirit will continue to shape the way you live, work, explore, and connect with the people around you. Being an artist isn't confined to a paycheck or a specific career path—it's woven into the way you express yourself and engage with the world. You're still an artist, even if your earnings don't come from acting.

If you're struggling with being a performer or artist right now, give yourself permission to change your mind—and see how that feels. Give yourself the freedom to find a new dance and see how that feels. Allow yourself to find a new rhythm, a new path, and see where it takes you.

The arts aren't going anywhere. The pandemic proved that. They are back, stronger than ever. So, if you need to step away for a while, know that you can always return—and you'll bring everything you've learned as an artist with you. Whatever new career path you choose, your experiences in the arts will continue to shape and guide you.

Are you experiencing burnout?

Do you feel it's time to shift gears and try something new? What would that be?

The Frame of Mind to Keep Working

More story time: I had an interview with a former student who was questioning whether he should continue acting. He was frustrated, thinking he wasn't as good as he used to be. As we unpacked his thoughts, we realized that during school, he was singing twenty-five+ hours a week, dancing five days a week from 8 to 9:30 a.m., and acting for three to four hours each day. After graduation, he started working immediately. His first job paid him a meager $100 a week, but he felt like he was living the dream.

Fast forward to after the pandemic, and with increased hours at his job to pay the bills, his routine had changed drastically. He stopped dancing, singing, and acting for forty+ hours a week, and with it came self-doubt about his abilities. When we talked, two key things emerged: First, it became clear that he couldn't be at the same physical level he was in school due to the balancing act of life and work as an adult. To get back to that level, he'd need to build a regular performance routine and start small. Based on his current schedule, he could sing at least one hour three times a week and attend two dance classes.

As we dug deeper, we also talked about the toll social media was taking on him. He realized he was comparing himself to others who had booked summer gigs. When we unpacked it further, he admitted that he had a direct offer of a job contract, but he had turned it down. His decision was based on his interest in the show, the financial loss of leaving his NYC job versus the pay of the gig, and whether the opportunity would advance his career.

By the end of our conversation, we both agreed that he still wanted to act, was capable of acting, and was booking work. He just needed to reframe his idea of what a career looks like as an adult and recalibrate the trajectory of his professional journey.

Framing your mindset around auditioning and self-tapes is crucial for persevering through the tough times. In a 2015 interview for the SAG-AFTRA Foundation, Michael Keaton shared a powerful realization about auditioning. He mentioned he had been approaching auditioning all wrong. Instead of auditioning to get the job, he understood that *auditioning* was the job itself. "I already got the job," he explained. "Whatever they're gonna' get me in a room, that's the gig. I got the job. I'm going to work today." Approach every audition and self-tape with the mindset of a freelance artist—it *is* your job for the day.

You're never done as an actor. There's always something more to learn and discover. If you feel that you've hit a wall in your career, I recommend you go back to class. A coach or a teacher can help you find where you're stuck and give you the tools to keep moving forward. It also supplies you with a network of other artists who're on the journey with you. Class is a place where you can recalibrate and reinvigorate your curiosity about your craft.

What do you need to recalibrate in order to move forward in your career?

What can you control or change today to keep moving forward?

How can you reinvigorate your curiosity about your craft?

2
The Business

Social Media

Social media has completely transformed our industry and is now an essential tool in shaping careers. It has the power to make or enhance a career. In 2005, YouTube was launched. By 2006, both X and Facebook became publicly available. In 2010, Instagram entered the scene, and influencers began gaining mainstream attention. TikTok followed in 2016, further changing the social media landscape. Today, the average person spends about two hours a day on social platforms.

For actors, this offers a unique opportunity. Regardless of the industry, anyone looking to hire will likely check out the social media profiles of potential candidates. That's why it's crucial to understand how your online presence is perceived.

My suggestion is to go find a computer that isn't yours and Google your own name. Then search for your name alongside each of your social media handles. What appears? You might be surprised by what shows up, especially when your computer's cookies aren't curating your results.

By reviewing your online footprint, you can ensure that the content you want to be seen is front and center. Having control over your digital image is essential—because what's online can stay online.

Mastering social media can benefit you in countless ways as an actor. It teaches you valuable skills like video editing, story framing, and even the art of curating costumes, lighting, and set design. As you create content, you'll become more comfortable in front of the camera, and you'll develop a deeper understanding of the creative process.

Social media also opens up opportunities like being the go-to person for Instagram takeovers when you're in a show, or building a personal brand that resonates with your audience. Challenge yourself to create new content each week; even if you don't post it, pushing yourself to produce content will build your confidence and skill set. If you're unsure where to start, don't worry—just Google it! There are endless ideas and resources out there to guide.

Decide for yourself how you want social media to serve your career. Is it a way to showcase your work, or a platform to reach a wider audience? Think about whether you want a personal account, a brand-focused account, or even both. It's also important to set boundaries—decide how much time and energy you're willing to invest in your social media presence. Use these platforms as tools to enhance your career, but don't let them control you. Always remember: Your worth isn't defined by the number of likes or followers you have. Social media can be a powerful tool to gain more interest in your product, but it does not define you.

As an outsider, what does your online presence say about you?

What do you want it to say about you?

What platforms do you gravitate toward?

How can you increase your online presence?

Branding

In today's industry, "branding" has become a buzzword, but it's much more than just a trend—it's a powerful tool for personal marketing. It's the way you define yourself in the industry, acting as a holistic stamp that claims, "This is who I am, and this is what I do." Your brand encompasses your essence, your look, your voice type, your material, your headshots, reel, audition book, and website. Two definitions of "essence" from *Webster* that really resonate with me are: "the intrinsic nature or indispensable quality of something, especially something abstract, that determines its character," and "the most significant element, quality, or aspect of a thing or person."

Your brand should be a clear, coherent statement that communicates to the world: **LOOK OUT, HERE I AM. THIS IS WHAT I DO WELL, AND THIS IS WHERE I FIT INTO THE INDUSTRY.**

Branding is something you should continually evaluate and adapt. As you grow and evolve, so too should your brand. The methods, tools, and platforms you use to shape your personal brand will naturally shift over time. Today, there are countless professionals who you can pay to help craft and refine a brand that truly represents you.

But if you don't want to spend money, below are some key questions that can help you get started on building your brand. These questions were developed through a collaboration between actress and professor Jennifer Hemphill and myself, during a 2020 presentation at the Musical Theatre Educators' Alliance.

As a Person:
- **What do I value in myself?**
  Reflect on your core values—what are the qualities you admire in yourself?

The Role You Play in Your Life:
- **What roles do you play in your social group, work, and family?**
  Consider how you show up in different areas of your life and how those roles might influence your brand.

Stories You Don't Want to Tell:
- **Identify five acting roles that don't resonate with you.**
- **What specific aspects of these roles do you find unappealing?**
- **What are the types of stories or roles you are not interested in telling?**

  This helps to clarify boundaries and identify what doesn't align with your personal or artistic values.

Stories You Want to Tell:
- **What type of stories do you want to tell, and why?**
- **What roles or genres are you most passionate about?**
- **What are your "dream roles," and why do they resonate with you?**

  Think about the stories you feel most drawn to and the reasons behind your passion for them.

Finding Your Essence:
- **Reflecting on the previous questions, what do you think is your intrinsic nature?**

  What unique qualities do you offer the world that no one else does? We all have many aspects of our essence, but what are the qualities that most often lead and define you?
- **Call a Friend:**

  Ask your friends and family to share what they believe are the key elements of your essence.
- **Collect Verbs:**

  Find verbs that describe your essence. Choose five verbs that truly capture what you offer and how you move through the world.

Name It/Claim It

Write down the leading element of your essence—the core quality or characteristic that defines you. Once you have a clear sense of who you are and what you offer, create a collage (either analog or digital) that visually represents all the elements of your essence.

When you have both the verbs that describe you and the visual representation of your essence, you can align all aspects of your professional presence—your website, reel, headshots, Actors Access, and resume—so they authentically reflect that essence.

Into the Void

One of the most significant shifts in our industry post-pandemic is the rise of self-submitted audition videos for theatre. While this practice has been standard in film and television for years, it became a necessity for theatres during the height of the COVID-19 pandemic. Thankfully, many first-round auditions and most callbacks are now back to in-person. However, mastering the art of self-taping is now a **requirement** for all actors.

Investing in the proper equipment to create high-quality self-submit audition videos can be a significant financial commitment. It's essential to have a good camera, proper lighting, clear sound, a clean background, and reliable editing tools. For those who may not have access to this equipment, many cities offer rental studios fully equipped for self-taping, where you can book a room with all the gear you need.

With the rise of self-taping and self-submission, actors from all over the world are now submitting for roles, leading to an overwhelming increase in the number of audition videos casting directors must review. One of the most difficult parts of this process is the feeling that your videos are being sent into a void with little to no response. Unlike in-person auditions, where you can gauge feedback and energy, self-taping offers no immediate connection or personal interaction. This can feel isolating and disheartening. However, cultivating a mindset of play and curiosity about improving your self-tapes can help ease this frustration. An actor I spoke with likened the process to Malcolm Gladwell's concept of the "10,000 hours"—a path to mastery of your craft. Each tape is an opportunity to improve, refine, and learn. With that mindset, the journey becomes one of growth, not just waiting for a response.

Below are some helpful tips and tricks from actors I've interviewed that can improve your self-submission videos.

- THE MOST IMPORTANT THING! Read the audition notice carefully and follow the instructions precisely. Only do what's requested in the breakdown to avoid over-delivering or missing the mark.
- From a casting director: **Respond to your ECO-Casting and label your files correctly!** Always read all the information provided to you and follow instructions to ensure you're submitting properly.
- Understand the reality: A director I spoke with mentioned that when reviewing thousands of auditions from an open call, she could often determine everything she needed to know from the slate alone. In fact, in many cases, she didn't watch past the slate because she could tell the actor wasn't right for the project based on their look, energy, or essence. This does not mean you should not do great takes. You never know what is being watched all the way through.
- Bank your slates. On a day when you're feeling and looking great, record all possible slates and body shots. This way, you'll have them ready to pull from whenever you need them.
- **Do the work!** Prepare for a self-tape audition with as much dedication as you would for an in-person audition. The camera knows when you haven't put in the effort—there's no faking it.
- Limit yourself to three to five takes and spend no more than twenty minutes per scene or song. Trying to create the perfect take can send you down an endless rabbit hole of revisions.
- Do one or two takes, then stop and review them. First, check to ensure the camera and sound are working properly. Next, watch with a critical eye to identify what's working and what needs improvement for the next take. This way, you're growing and refining with each attempt.
- Watch your takes without sound. This allows you to assess whether you're truly telling the story through your actions, or if you're relying too much on the dialogue to communicate your meaning.
- If the deadline isn't immediate, don't rush to choose a take. Give yourself some time and perspective (a few hours or even a day) before revisiting the footage. This break will allow you to come back with fresh eyes.
- Most people hate watching themselves on camera. Be kind to yourself when reviewing your takes. If you're struggling to choose or can't bear to watch, ask a trusted friend to help pick the best one for you.
- Be completely memorized. It's incredibly obvious in self-tapes if you're not fully off-book. Be memorized and, if you are singing, have a Bluetooth speaker.

- **Find the right reader.** Make sure they're not overpowering the audition with their volume and that they understand this is *your* audition, not theirs.

Which of the above practices do you want to implement?

Do you need to upgrade or improve your self-tape setup?

The Crowded Market

As part of my research for this book, I participated in several unified auditions in the NY/NJ region. Unified auditions are structured as a ninety-second package format, where you present your material to a room full of representatives from twenty to thirty theatres at once. Most audition packages consist of either two songs or a monologue and a song or two monologues.

It's basically a cattle call.

I had the unique opportunity to experience one of these auditions from both sides of the table. I participated as an actor, while also serving as a casting representative for the summer theatre program affiliated with Kent State University. For this specific unified audition, there was a "prescreening," if you passed the prescreening, you were then invited to attend the summer stock auditions—either in person or virtually.

During the in-person audition weekend, it was reported that we saw *over* 1,500 actors just in the musical theatre room. The following weekend, we saw an additional 1,000 actors virtually. As part of my research for this book, I had the opportunity to interview someone behind the scenes who coordinates this annual event. When I asked how many people nationally auditioned for the prescreening process, I was told the number was around 9,000 total that year. So, to put that into perspective, 9,000 people auditioning for 2,500 available audition "slots," which in turn lead to 300–500 acting jobs across 20–30 theatre companies.

The oversaturation of the market is real. According to a study by Queen Mary University of London, only "2% of actors make a living from acting, while 90% are out of work at any given time." This underscores the importance of understanding what makes you unique. Go back to the "Branding" section and reflect upon what you bring to the audition room that is distinctly yours.

What makes you unique?

What sets you apart in the audition room?

The Book

Thankfully, most EPA (Equity Principal Auditions) and ECC (Equity Choirs Calls) and nonequity tour auditions are now in-person. In a time with Pop Icons are staring in movie musicals like *Wicked* and making their Broadway debuts, having an audition book that reflects these changing times is important. Pop Rock is a must-have for your audition book.

Creating Your Audition Book: Your audition book is a three-ring binder of 16-to-32-bar song cuts (roughly one minute in length). It's also a good idea to include a few 8-bar cuts for flexibility in different audition settings. When selecting songs, be sure to choose material that you love to sing and that it falls within your vocal range, your demographic, and your age range—ideally, roles that are three to five years above or below your age. It's also essential to have a digital backup of your book. This will give you more choices in the audition room if needed and make sure that if you lose your book, you have a backup.

Some possible categories for your book include the following:
Traditional Book Musical
- One up-tempo
- One ballad
Contemporary
- Up-tempo
- Ballad or power ballad

Pop/Rock
- One or two that would fit 1950s and 1960s
- One or two that would fit 1970s and 1980s
- One or two that would fit 1990s and early 2000s
- One or two current pop/rock
- One country and western
- One R&B

When approaching pop/rock, it is important to find pop/rock music that really speaks to you. Telling a story while singing is important, but embodying the essence of the pop/rock song will help you stand out.

Ways to Discover New Material

1. **The Deep Dive:** Start by selecting a Broadway role that aligns with your vocal range and type. Depending on your age, this could even be a role in the ensemble. Research the performer who originated the role and explore other characters they've played. From there, look into who else has portrayed that role and investigate the other parts they've taken on. This process helps you gain insight into potential roles you could play and gives you a clearer understanding of your casting possibilities.

2. **Exploring Pop/Rock:** Start by browsing playlists on your preferred streaming platform. Choose an era and find a playlist that features your voice range and explore songs that resonate with you. This can be a fun way to discover new material that feels authentic to your voice.

Finding the right audition song takes time and patience. Make it a game! Challenge yourself to explore new artists and genres and see how many new songs you can discover that might be a great fit for your next audition.

What do you feel is missing from you audition book?

Which songs no longer resonate with you and should be removed?

Truth of Casting: It's Not Personal

Casting is not personal, and it's not about you. Your job is to do your best work and leave it in the room. This was the hardest concept for me to grasp in the early stages of becoming an actor. I didn't fully comprehend this notion until I started directing. From a director's point of view, we're trying to create a complete puzzle, and, you, the actor, are a singular puzzle piece. There are many moving parts that go into casting. Actors in general have almost no control over these parts. A great analogy I once heard compared casting to shopping. When you go to a store to buy a new black dress, how do you pick? Let's say you find four great dresses, they all fit, they're all black, and they're high in quality. How do you pick the dress? It might be because you know the designer of the dress and you like their work, you trust their work, and you know it will be a reliable dress. You might base it on the fact that the specific shade of black fits perfect with the shoes you want to wear. You might base it on a feeling. There are so many reasons for you to pick the black dress that aren't a reflection of the dress's integrity and worth. After evaluating all the dresses, you pick one and leave the others behind. There is nothing wrong with the dresses left behind; you might also take pictures of them so you have a reference because you know you might need them in the future

This is how casting works. The Director picks the cast based on not only the needs of that role but also, frankly, on arbitrary things. How does this actor look in the costume? Do they fit the picture that we're trying to create? Have they worked with the director before? Regardless, your job is to keep showing up, be prepared, and be a joy in the room. After that, you have limited control over why you're cast or not cast.

Please note—casting is slowly changing. More inclusive casting practices are coming into play. As an industry, we still have a long way to go until casting is truly equitable. (See the section, "**The Industry Is Changing,**" for more detail.)

Are their audition or situations you need to depersonalize?

How will knowing this help you walk into your next audition?

Do the Hustle

Let's just be upfront—the hustle of this industry looks different than it did five years ago. It's necessary to find new ways to get in front of casting. *Actors Access* (https://actorsaccess.com/) and *Casting Network* (https://www.casting-networks.com) are THE go-to place for theatre, film, and television auditions. A completed Actors Access and Casting Network page is now the equivalent of a well-put-together audition book. (This includes headshot, resume, and media). The Hustle NYC is also another place where you can pay to get a calendar of where and when all the auditions are happening. Other helpful platforms to find auditions are *Backstage, Actors Equity*, and *Playbill*. Please know that you have to pay to be on these audition platforms. This is an investment that will be invaluable to your future as an actor!

There are websites like *Up To Date Actor* that compile auditions from across the country, allowing you to search by role or region to find opportunities that are right for you. Additionally, there are companies such as *Growing Studio, Actors Connection,* and *One on One NYC* that offer paid services to help you get in front of casting directors and agents.

If you choose to invest in a class to meet industry professionals, be strategic about your decision. Know why you're taking the class and what you hope to achieve. If there's a specific show or project you believe you're perfect for, and the class is within your budget, it can be a valuable opportunity. Always evaluate the cost–benefit ratio before committing to any class or service designed to connect you with industry insiders.

Staying informed about what's happening in the industry is essential. I recommend dedicating a part of your morning reading trade publications. For Los Angeles, *Variety* and *The Hollywood Reporter* are key sources, while in New York, *Playbill* and *Broadway Briefing* are invaluable.

It's also a good idea to spend the first part of your day self-submitting and researching upcoming auditions. This proactive approach helps you take control of your career and ensures you're staying on top of opportunities.

If you choose to attend open calls as a nonequity actor, it's important to understand that you may not always be seen. However, always bring your complete audition book, along with several copies of your headshot and resume. In New York City, many auditions take place in the same few blocks. If you don't think you'll be seen for one show, don't hesitate to cross the street and try for another audition. Staying flexible and open to new opportunities is key.

A Reminder: You don't have to attend every audition. Focus on the ones that are right for you—those that align with your strengths and the stories you're passionate about telling. Many people I've interviewed have shared that they burned themselves out in their first couple of years in the city by trying to attend *every* audition, rather than being more strategic about where they focused their effort.

Are your Actors Access and Casting Network profiles up to date?

Are you a member of other audition platforms?

Do you make it a priority to read the trades and submit to auditions every morning?

Unions and Representation

The performing arts industry is made up of various unions and guilds that represent different sectors. On Broadway, there are thirteen unions and guilds, while in film and television, nineteen unions and guilds work together. As an actor, the two major unions are:

- **Actors' Equity Association (AEA):** for theatre
- **Screen Actors Guild—American Federation of Television and Radio Artists (SAG-AFTRA):** for film, television, and other media.

When and how to join the union is a personal decision that varies for each actor. There are different pathways to union membership depending on the union.

For AEA, there are three ways to join:
1. **Through being a member of an affiliate performers' union**
2. **Being in employment under an equity contract**
3. **Through the Open Access program**

For SAG-AFTRA, there are typically two ways to join:
1. **By working as a background actor or principal performer on a SAG-AF-TRA production**
2. **Through membership in an affiliate performers' union**

When to Join the Union

For actors just starting out, gaining experience as a nonunion performer may be more beneficial than joining the union immediately. The choice to join should take into account your personal career goals and the market and area you're working in. Be sure to do your research and talk to trusted members of your community to understand the benefits and drawbacks of joining at different stages in your career. Every actor's journey to union membership is unique. Every actor I interviewed had their own stories of how and why they joined.

Agents and Managers

Your agent only gets 10% of your paycheck because they only do 10% of your work. Yes, having an agent can open doors to auditions that might otherwise be out of reach, but many actors, especially in theatre, have launched successful careers without one. I especially see it in my own students. At the conclusion of their senior showcase, many expect that "making it" is determined if they get signed by an agent. This is not true!

I've had students who landed an agent immediately but didn't book a single job for years. Conversely, I've had others who didn't sign with an agent but went on to book national tours on their own within a year.

If you want to find an agent or manager, there are several ways to successfully do so:
1. **Showcases:** Whether through a college or paid showcases, these events can be an opportunity to connect with agents.

2. **Research**: Take the time to research agencies that align with your career goals and reach out directly.
3. **Doing the Work**: Consistently audition, excel in your roles, and invite people to see your performances—word-of-mouth can be powerful.
4. **Content Creation**: Create your own work or showcases and invite agents and managers to see the performances firsthand.
5. **Referrals**: Do such excellent work on set or in your show that people recommend you to their agent.

Understanding the Difference between an Agent and a Manager

I know many actors who've started their careers with a manager instead of an agent, or vice versa. It's important to understand the roles and differences between the two.

An agent is licensed in the state they operate and can submit you for work or auditions, as well as negotiate contracts. Most reputable agents work in alignment with the actor's union and are legally limited to taking a 10% commission. Agents want you to book work and will submit you for any job you're right for and have a larger client roster. Depending on the agency's size, you may have separate agents for different areas of work, such as commercial, theatrical, or film/television, or a single agent who manages all these areas.

A manager is *not* licensed in a state and legally shouldn't be able to submit you for work or negotiate contracts. However, in the real world it doesn't work this way. Any manager worth their salt will be submitting you for auditions. Managers have a smaller roster and should curate the full career trajectory of their actors. For example, they might suggest you take or don't take a contract depending on where you want your long-term career to go. Since managers are not licensed to a certain state, they will take a 10%–20% commission on any job you book. Most managers negotiate a 15% commission.

The most important thing is you should NEVER pay for an agent or a manager. They only get paid when you book work. You should never pay someone to submit you for auditions. Selecting the right agent and manager is a personal journey. You will want one who understands your vision of your career and pushes you.

Good work begets good work. Make sure anything you put out to the public is your best work at that moment. If you're contacting agent/managers, casting agents, or directors, keep the emails short and professional and have links to your Actors Access profile and your website in the email. Blanket mass emails are frowned upon. Do your research and reach out to the people and projects you know you're right for. You can find so much information online now, so take the time to do the research before you submit anything to anyone. Don't be afraid to contact someone (professionally) for a project you feel you're right for. The worst thing that can happen is you don't hear anything.

If you're not currently represented, what steps are you taking to pursue representation?

Kill Them with Kindness

Over the last decade plus of teaching, I have brought in working professionals from all aspects of the industry to speak to my students. What is the number one piece of advice they all share? Be kind, be talented, and be reliable. Attitude, gossip, and an inflated ego can quickly derail a career.

I had a friend who worked at a major casting office, where their role was to monitor the audition room and manage the order of auditioners. They were a vital part of the casting process, not just for logistics, but because they kept track of who was courteous—and who wasn't. For almost every project they worked on, they would eliminate actors from consideration on the sole basis of how respectful (or not) they were of others. People in charge of casting take notice.

I was recently directing a show and had to choose between an unknown actor and someone I had worked with before. The reading of this unknown actor was maybe "better" than the actor I knew, BUT the actor I knew is a joy to have in the room. They bring out the best in everyone around them—they're kind, on time, curious, and take direction well. You can probably guess who I cast: the actor I knew. That being said, I still have the other actor's information on file, and if a future project calls for their skill set, I will absolutely bring them in.

Reference checks happen! Over the past fifteen years as a director, I've been contacted numerous times to provide references for actors who've worked with me. Professional companies want to know that you're not only talented but also a good person. Conversely, I've had other directors reach out to me to ask if I had the same negative experience with an actor, knowing neither of us would hire them again. This industry is small—one degree of separation is very real. So, be someone who's a joy to have in the room, and you'll keep working.

It bears repeating, but there is a fine line between confidence and arrogance. One is knowing what you know because you have put the time, effort, and dedication into honing your craft, and the other is your ego trying to prove that you're inherently better than everyone else in the room.

Are you a joy to have in the room?

Do you have a strong work ethic?

What can you change to become the person people want to keep working with?

Money, Money, Money

The entertainment industry is a multibillion-dollar industry. In 2023, the combined gross revenue of Broadway, film, and television properties in the United States is estimated to be around $175 billion. We may think that artists make up the entertainment industry, but the truth is that it is run by heads of business. Understanding the financial structure of the entertainment industry will help you gain perspective on what role an actor plays in this corporate entertainment industry machine. Actors are important, but ultimately, they are a cog in the wheel of a gigantic machine.

Looking at budget breakdowns of Broadway musicals and major films and television shows, actor's salaries make up only about 8%–16% of the budget. This means that 84%–92% of the budget goes to other aspects of building the "product." This includes advertising, building set construction, lights, costumes, union compensation, directors, authors, rehearsal space, rent for the theatre, front of house, shooting locations, cost of the cameras, special effects, editing, and much more. Casting is important, but, ultimately, actors are replaceable in the grand scheme of any show or production. *Therefore, being on time, reliable, kind, and doing good solid work is imperative to being cast and getting cast again.*

In a Queen Mary University study 2019, it is stated that only 2% of actors worldwide make a living acting and 90% of actors are out of work at any given time. The Screen Actors Guild—American Federation of Television and Radio Artists (SAG/AFTRA) represents approximately 160,000 actors, and Actors Equity Association (AEA) has approximately 51,000 members.

In 2024, the SAG-AFTRA weekly rate for a large budget film is $4,546.80, while a low-budget film pays around $1,282 per week. For ultra-low-budget films or SAG student films, the weekly rate is often negotiated but can range from $500 to $700. For Broadway, the AEA weekly contract is $2,323, and, for Off-Broadway, rates range from $800 to $1,250 per week, depending on the contract. A development agreement contract for workshops of new musicals or plays can pay anywhere from $200 to $700 per week. For a special appearance AEA contract, the rate starts around $400 per week.

In 2024, New York, NY state and federal taxes are roughly 28% of your salary (depending on your income). To illustrate this deduction, let's look at an AEA Broadway production league contract. If your pay is $2,323 a week, your take-home pay would be around $1,660. An agent, if you have one, will take 10%, and, a manager, if you have one, will take another 10%–15% depending on your contract. Therefore, your take-home salary would be between $1,080 and $1,400 per week depending on your representation. In Los Angeles, CA, the state and federal taxes are 21.2% of your salary (depending on your income). A weekly SAG big budget film compensation of $4,546.80 per week would ultimately equate to a take-home pay of $3,583. If you had both an agent and manager, your take-home compensation would be around $2,688 a week. Please note that the tax rate changes from year to year.

Understanding this can help you identify other jobs that will support your livelihood. As Elizabeth Gilbert wisely says in *Big Magic*: "Don't make your art pay for your life." This perspective can alleviate the pressure of believing that success in the industry means relying solely on acting to cover all your bills. It also helps put things into perspective: While actors are crucial to the industry, they are not its driving force. Actors may be the most visible component, but they are just one piece in a much larger puzzle.

What are some other jobs you can successfully pursue while performing?

Does learning about the financial side of the industry change the way you view your role in it?

The Industry Is Changing

Very slowly, but steadily, equity and diversity in casting and creating teams are expanding. Per the UCLA-Hollywood-Diversity report for Film and TV, for the year 2024, 4.5 out of every 10 lead actors are people of color. Women played leads 51% of the time compared only to the figure of 25.3% in 2013. For Film and TV directors, "3.1 out of every 10 directors" were people of color and "3.1 out of every 10 film directors were woman." These numbers have increased since 2022.

According to the Actors' Equity Association's 2021 report on Hiring Bias and Wage Gaps in Theatre (published in 2023), the percentage of roles filled by BI-POC (Black, Indigenous, People of Color) actors increased from 21.3% in 2016 to 28.6% in 2021. In 2024, 25 musicals on Broadway employed Black actors. During the COVID shutdown of Broadway from 2020 to 2022, the Broadway community made a concerted effort to increase the representation of BIPOC actors, directors, designers, writers, producers, and individuals in leadership positions. While progress has been made, there's still room for improvement.

For example, in the 2022–2023 Broadway season, only 17% of shows were written by people of color. In the 2023–2024 season, about 25% of Broadway shows were directed by women, but only around 11% were directed by people of color. In another important breakthrough, *How to Dance in Ohio* (2023) became the first musical ever to feature a fully neurodivergent cast.

This industry is slowly evolving to reflect the diverse mix of people, stories, and talents that we see on stage and on screen. It is through the diligence and advocacy of artists that we continue to push for the belief that every story deserves to be told, and all people should be represented in the arts.

How can you contribute to advancing diverse stories?

Creating Your Own Work

Looking at the current state of representation—or the lack thereof—on stage, in film, and on television—if you don't see the stories that reflect you, GO CREATE YOUR OWN WORK. Don't wait for someone else to do it—take matters into your own hands! If you don't write, direct, or produce, find people who do. Tell the stories that resonate with you. Take control of what's being said and how it's being told.

Like it often happens in any creative endeavor, your first project might not be any good and that's okay. Keep pushing. There are countless unique voices in the performing arts that our culture would never have been exposed to, had those creators given up after their first attempt.

Creating your own content is a way to take ownership of your career instead of waiting for someone to give you permission. Grab your phone or computer, and make a five-minute film. Write a short play and perform it in your living room, at your local community center, or church. Start small, experiment, and see where it takes you.

I've seen it firsthand: I supported a student who wrote a short play for a student theatre festival, and, through their hard work and perseverance, their play performed Off-Broadway. Another student created a short film that was selected for both local and national film festivals.

It is in the creation of the work where you have the say.

> What stories do you want to tell?
>
> Create a five-minute play or film—what can you learn from this?
>
> How do you plan to take full control of your career moving forward?

Conclusion

After interviewing actors, directors, producers, agents, and managers, one thing is clear: *No one's journey in this industry is the same.* Only you get to say what your version of success is. The beautiful thing about success is the definition of it changes and evolves as you do. The dreams and goals you have now may not be the same ones you hold in twenty years, BUT THE QUESTIONING NEVER STOPS. The ongoing exploration of who you are, both as a person and an actor, is a journey that never truly ends.

There is HONOR in the journey of becoming a storyteller, regardless of whether you "make it." You can make a meaningful impact as an artist at any level—whether you're working with your local community theatre or in a major city. Only you can decide WHY you choose to stay in the arts.

This industry is magic, as defined by *Merriam-Webster*: "an extraordinary power or influence seemingly from a supernatural source." I believe there's a force within us that drives us to keep going—not to "make it" but simply to create!

There are no guarantees in this industry, but the journey is worth taking. You will discover something about yourself on the road ahead. Enjoy the gift that pursuing your dream will give you. Remember, whether you choose to pursue a career as an actor or find fulfillment performing at your local community theatre, both paths are valid! What matters most is the expression of your soul. No one can tell you that you are not worthy to pursue what brings you joy and what you love.

Now go, create, and live your most resilient life!!!

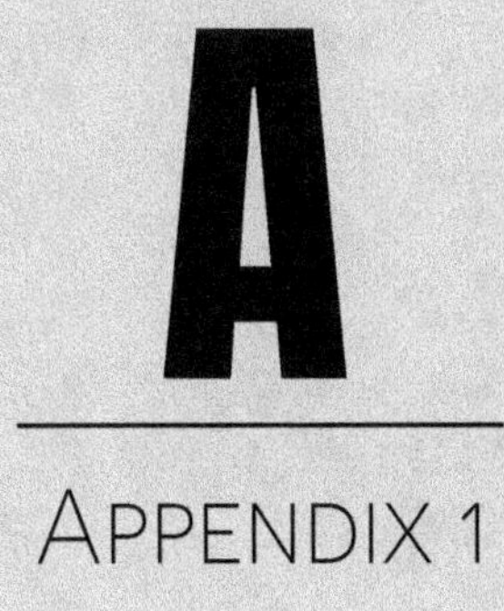

Sample Resume

Acting resumes should be printed on a single side of an 8x10 sheet of paper.

YOUR NAME
AEA/SAG-AFTRA
Website

Cellphone	Height
Email	Vocal Range
Ethnicity (ex: Latine)	and/or Gender or Pronouns

TV

Name of Show	Series Regular	Name of Network or Chan./Name of Dir
Name of Show	Recurring	Name of Network or Chan./Name of Dir
Name of Show	Guest Start	Name of Network or Chan./Name of Dir
Name of Show	Co-Start	Name of Network or Chan./Name of Dir

FILM

Name of Film	Lead	Dir: Name of Director
Name of Film	Supporting Role	Dir: Name of Director
Name of Film	Lead	Dir: Name of Director

THEATRE

Name of Show	Name of Role	Name of Theatre/Dir: If well known
Name of Show	Swing/Dance Captain	Name of Theatre/Dir: If well known
Name of Show	U/S Lead role (w/perfs)	Name of Theatre/Dir: If well known

EDUCATIONAL THEATRE

Name of Show	Name of Role	Name of School Dir: if known in NYC
Name of Show	Name of Role	Name of School Dir: if known in NYC

COMMERCIALS/VOICEOVER/INDUSTRIALS

List upon Request

EDUCATION/TRAINING

BA or BFA in Acting, XXX University, Graduation Date XXXX
Acting: Name of Teacher, Years of Study
Singing:
Dancing:
On-Camera

SKILLS

Languages, Accents, Sports, Unique Talents (Learn to Juggle)